Midnight Spaghetti

WILFRID SHEED
OFFICE POLITICS
McNALLY EDITIONS

Midnight Spaghetti

Effortless pasta
20 minutes
5 ingredients
No fuss

Caroline Griffiths

Smith Street Books

Contents

Introduction

Let's be honest: dinner is not always a grand production. Maybe it's a Wednesday night and you're tired, or it's midnight and you're hungry, or you just want a bowl of something hot and comforting that doesn't ask too much of you. That's where this book comes in.

Midnight Spaghetti is about keeping things simple – five ingredients or fewer (not counting the pasta, oil of some kind, salt or pepper, because let's be real, these pantry staples don't count). Every recipe is designed to be made in 20 minutes or less, which means no simmering for hours, no complicated prep, no scrolling for substitutions. Just fast, unfussy, excellent food that delivers way more than the sum of its parts.

Pasta is a brilliant solution to most dinner conundrums. It's inexpensive, it's forgiving and it's endlessly adaptable. With just a handful of other ingredients – sun-dried tomatoes, a spoonful of miso paste, maybe a splash of sriracha – you can build something that feels like a proper meal without draining your energy (or your bank account).

The recipes in this book lean into bold flavours to deliver dishes that feel a little indulgent, but are secretly very easy with a few clever shortcuts. Smoked trout with lemon. Carbonara with guanciale. Creamy pumpkin and leek. Plus a few new favourites with a decidedly cosmopolitan twist, including Sichuan chilli pork or beef bulgogi with spinach and sesame seeds. You can cook these delicious dishes for friends and call it dinner, or enjoy them solo straight from the pot while standing in your kitchen. No judgement.

Think of this book as your late-night companion, your weeknight saviour, your Sunday comfort. Food for when you want to feel pampered without putting in much effort – food that makes being hungry at midnight feel like a sneaky gourmet opportunity.

About the recipes

Although this book is called *Midnight Spaghetti,* it could just as easily be called *Midnight Fettucine* or *Midnight Bucatini.* That is to say, feel free to swap out spaghetti for whatever other long pasta variety you happen to have in your pantry. Spaghettini, linguine, tagliatelle, mafaldine – go for it.

All the recipes call for 'dried spaghetti', but not all pastas are created equal. If you can, seek out 'bronze-cut' or 'bronze-extruded' varieties. These are made using a more artisanal method of cutting pasta which produces a rough, porous surface – allowing your sauces to better cling to and coat the pasta strands for the most mouth-pleasing results.

The recipes use 15 ml (1/2 fl oz) tablespoon measures.

Cooking pasta

Bring 1.5–2 litres (6–8 cups) water to the boil in a large saucepan over high heat, with the lid on. (You need less water than you think – concentrating the starch that gets released from the pasta into the cooking water helps later on in the cooking process, bringing the sauce together to silky perfection.)

Add about 2 teaspoons of salt and your spaghetti to the saucepan. Using a wooden spoon or long-handled tongs, mix the spaghetti as it softens and collapses into the pan. Cover with the lid again for about 1 minute, to bring the water back to the boil quickly, then follow the recipe instructions as directed.

No oil in pasta water, please!

Don't waste good olive oil by adding it to your pan of boiling water to cook your pasta. The oil won't stop the spaghetti sticking together – instead, use the correct amount of water and a wooden spoon or long-handled tongs to stir the pasta as it collapses into the pan. Oil in the water can coat the pasta, creating a barrier that hinders your lovingly created sauce from clinging to the spaghetti perfectly. Save your olive oil for cooking the sauce or drizzling on at the end.

Grating cheese

When adding hard cheese, like parmesan or pecorino romano, directly to your frying pan to create a creamy sauce, use the finest grater you have – a microplane is ideal. Very finely grated cheese will melt quickly into the sauce without clumping.

SANGIOVESE

Classics

CORLEONE
CORLEONE
PRODUCED WITH ORGANIC ANCIENT GRAINS FROM SICILY
SPAGHETTI N°5
SPAGHETTI
EXTRA VIRGIN OLIVE OIL
RISERVA

Spaghetti amatriciana

Salty pancetta, fiery chilli, tangy tomato – this is the late-night pasta you'll keep coming back to. Amatriciana is Roman comfort food at its best: simple, bold, a little messy, and exactly what you want after a long day (or night). The sauce comes together while your pasta cooks, and a snowfall of pecorino ties it all together. Midnight cravings? Handled.

Serves 2

200 g (7 oz) dried spaghetti
1 tablespoon extra virgin olive oil
150 g (5½ oz) pancetta, cut into 5–6 mm (¼ in) thick matchsticks
2 tablespoons tomato paste (concentrated puree)
½–1 teaspoon chilli flakes, to taste
400 g (14 oz) tin Italian roma (plum) tomatoes, whole or crushed
40 g (½ cup) very finely grated pecorino romano, plus extra to serve

1. Cook the spaghetti in a large saucepan of boiling salted water for about 3 minutes less than specified on the packet, until slightly underdone and less than al dente. Drain.

2. Meanwhile, combine the olive oil and pancetta in a deep 28 cm (11 in) unheated frying pan, stirring to coat the pancetta with the oil. Cook over medium heat for 6–8 minutes, until the fat renders and becomes translucent. Add the tomato paste and chilli and cook, stirring, for a further 2 minutes.

3. Add the tomatoes to the pan, breaking them up with a spoon if they are whole (or with your hands before adding, if you like). Simmer for 5–8 minutes, until slightly thickened, stirring occasionally.

4. Add the spaghetti and toss well to completely coat the pasta, shaking the pan and stirring with a wooden spoon. Remove from the heat, cover the pan and set aside for 1–2 minutes to allow the spaghetti to finish cooking and to absorb some of the sauce.

5. Stir in the cheese until melted and combined. Taste and season with freshly ground black pepper and salt, if necessary.

6. Divide between warmed serving bowls or plates and serve with extra pecorino, if you like.

Cacio e pepe

Here's proof that pasta doesn't need a long ingredient list to be iconic: just spaghetti, olive oil, black pepper, pecorino and a little kitchen magic. Creamy, peppery, deeply satisfying – and yes, somehow it always feels fancier than the 15 minutes or so it takes to pull together. A pasta worth twirling dramatically, preferably late at night with a glass of wine.

Serves 2

200 g (7 oz) dried spaghetti
2 tablespoons extra virgin olive oil, plus extra to drizzle
1 teaspoon fresh coarsely ground black pepper, plus extra to serve
80 g (1 cup) very finely grated pecorino romano (see Tips), plus extra to serve

1. Cook the spaghetti in a large saucepan of boiling salted water for about 3 minutes less than specified on the packet, until slightly underdone and less than al dente. Do not drain.

2. About 5 minutes before the spaghetti is ready, heat the olive oil and pepper in a deep 28 cm (11 in) frying pan over medium heat for 2–3 minutes, swirling the pan regularly, until the pepper is fragrant.

3. Add about 125 ml (1/2 cup) of the pasta water to the pan. Using tongs, add the spaghetti to the peppery oil in the frying pan, straight from the saucepan. Cook for 2–3 minutes, shaking the pan and moving the spaghetti around with a wooden spoon to finish cooking the spaghetti, help release more starch from the pasta and emulsify the sauce. Add more pasta water if the pan dries out – a small amount of liquid should remain in the pan to help form the sauce.

4. When the pasta is al dente, either remove the pan from the heat and set aside for about 1 minute to cool slightly, or tip the pasta into a large warmed bowl.

5. Meanwhile, stir a small amount of the slightly cooled pasta water into the grated pecorino with a fork to form a slurry. Add to the spaghetti with an extra drizzle of olive oil. Swirl the pan or bowl, stirring gently but quickly until a creamy sauce forms. Taste and add a little extra freshly ground black pepper.

6. Divide between warmed serving bowls or plates and serve with extra pecorino and more pepper, if you like.

Tips

Finely grate the cheese with a microplane so that it melts quickly into the sauce without clumping.

Pecorino romano can be quite sharp; to soften the flavour slightly, swap out half the pecorino for finely grated parmesan.

Garlic, olive oil & chilli spaghetti

If pasta had a party trick, this would be it. Just garlic, olive oil, chilli and a little heat, and suddenly spaghetti turns into something craveable, cosy, and way more than the sum of its parts. A quick handful of parsley keeps things fresh, and the whole dish practically demands a second helping. It's just as good at noon as it is at midnight.

Serves 2

200 g (7 oz) dried spaghetti
60 ml (1/4 cup) extra virgin olive oil
3 garlic cloves, finely sliced
1 small red chilli, sliced, or 1/2 teaspoon chilli flakes
small handful chopped flat-leaf parsley, plus extra to serve

1. Cook the spaghetti in a large saucepan of boiling salted water for about 3 minutes less than specified on the packet, until slightly underdone and less than al dente. Scoop out and reserve 250 ml (1 cup) of the pasta water and drain the pasta.

2. About 5 minutes before the spaghetti is ready, combine the olive oil, garlic and chilli in a deep 28 cm (11 in) unheated frying pan, stirring to coat the garlic and chilli with the oil. Cook over medium heat for 2–3 minutes, swirling the pan regularly, until the garlic is fragrant and just starts to turn golden.

3. Add about 80 ml (1/3 cup) of the reserved pasta water, along with the spaghetti, parsley and a pinch of salt. Toss well to coat the pasta, shaking the pan and stirring with a wooden spoon for a further 1–2 minutes, to finish cooking the spaghetti and to emulsify the pan juices and pasta water. Add a little more pasta water if the mixture seems dry. Taste and season with salt and freshly ground black pepper.

4. Divide between warmed serving bowls, scatter with extra parsley and serve.

Spaghetti carbonara

This is the queen of late-night pasta: rich, silky and indulgent, without being fussy. Guanciale (or pancetta) lays the smoky, salty foundation; eggs and cheese whisk into a sauce that clings to every strand of spaghetti. This is the kind of dish you can throw together quickly but still brag about later. Extra parmesan is a must.

Serves 2

200 g (7 oz) dried spaghetti
1 tablespoon extra virgin olive oil
120 g (4½ oz) guanciale (see Tips) or pancetta, skin removed, cut into thick matchsticks
60 g (¾ cup) very finely grated parmesan (see Tips), plus extra to serve
1 egg
2 egg yolks
½ teaspoon fresh coarsely ground black pepper, plus extra to serve
small handful chopped flat-leaf parsley, to serve (optional)

1. Cook the spaghetti in a large saucepan of boiling salted water for about 3 minutes less than specified on the packet, until slightly underdone and less than al dente. Do not drain.

2. Meanwhile, combine the olive oil and guanciale or pancetta in a deep 28 cm (11 in) unheated frying pan, stirring to coat the meat with the oil. Cook over medium heat for 8–10 minutes, until the fat renders and becomes translucent, and the meat starts to brown and crisp. Add about 125 ml (½ cup) of the pasta water to the pan.

3. Combine the parmesan, egg, egg yolks and pepper in a bowl, mixing with a fork to form a slurry. Set aside.

4. Using tongs, add the spaghetti to the frying pan, straight from the saucepan. Cook for 1–2 minutes, shaking the pan and moving the spaghetti around with a wooden spoon to finish cooking the spaghetti, help release more starch from the pasta and emulsify the sauce.

5. When the pasta is al dente, either remove the pan from the heat and set aside for 1–2 minutes to cool slightly, or tip the pasta into a large warmed bowl.

6. Add the cheese and egg mixture. Swirl the pan or bowl, stirring gently but quickly until a creamy sauce forms. Add a little more pasta water if the sauce needs thinning. Taste and season with extra pepper and salt, if necessary.

7. Divide between warmed serving bowls and serve with extra parmesan and parsley, if you like.

Tips

Guanciale is salt-cured and aged pork cheek, Italian in origin. It is available from good delicatessens and specialty butchers.

Finely grate the cheese with a microplane so that it melts quickly into the sauce without clumping.

Spaghetti gricia

Carbonara without the eggs, amatriciana without the tomato and chilli – gricia is the understated Roman classic that deserves more love. It's all about good guanciale, sharp pecorino and a hit of black pepper. Simple, salty and luxurious in that 'I only used five ingredients but look at me' kind of way, it's a true late-night win.

Serves 2

200 g (7 oz) dried spaghetti
1 tablespoon extra virgin olive oil
100 g (3½ oz) guanciale (see Tips, page 22) or pancetta, skin removed, cut into thick matchsticks
½ teaspoon fresh coarsely ground black pepper, plus extra to serve
40 g (½ cup) very finely grated pecorino romano (see Tips, page 22), plus extra to serve

1. Cook the spaghetti in a large saucepan of boiling salted water for about 3 minutes less than specified on the packet, until slightly underdone and less than al dente. Do not drain.

2. Meanwhile, combine the olive oil and guanciale or pancetta in a deep 28 cm (11 in) unheated frying pan, stirring to coat the meat with the oil. Cook over medium heat for 8–10 minutes, until the fat renders and becomes translucent, and the meat starts to brown and crisp.

3. Add about 125 ml (½ cup) of the pasta water to the pan. Using tongs, add the spaghetti to the frying pan, straight from the saucepan. Add the pepper and cook for 2–3 minutes, shaking the pan and moving the spaghetti around with a wooden spoon to finish cooking the spaghetti, help release more starch from the pasta and emulsify the sauce. Add more pasta water if the pan dries out – a small amount of liquid should remain in the pan to help form the sauce.

4. When the pasta is al dente, either remove the pan from the heat and set aside for 1–2 minutes to cool slightly, or tip the pasta into a large warmed bowl.

5. Stir a small amount of the slightly cooled pasta water into the grated pecorino with a fork to form a slurry. Add to the spaghetti mixture. Swirling the pan or bowl, stir gently but quickly to melt the cheese, until a creamy sauce forms. Add a little more pasta water if the sauce needs thinning. Taste and season with extra pepper and salt, if necessary.

6. Divide between warmed serving bowls and serve with extra pecorino, if you like.

Spaghetti puttanesca

This one's bold, briny and a little chaotic – anchovies, olives, capers, garlic and tomatoes all fighting for attention, and somehow winning. Punchy, salty and more than a little saucy, it's exactly what you need when you're hungry and impatient.

Serves 2

200 g (7 oz) dried spaghetti
2 tablespoons extra virgin olive oil
2 garlic cloves, finely chopped
4 good-quality anchovy fillets in olive oil, drained and chopped
400 g (14 oz) tin Italian roma (plum) tomatoes, whole or crushed
80 g (1/2 cup) pitted black olives, torn in half
2 tablespoons capers, rinsed well if salted

1. Cook the spaghetti in a large saucepan of boiling salted water for about 3 minutes less than specified on the packet, until slightly underdone and less than al dente. Drain.

2. Meanwhile, combine the olive oil, garlic and anchovies in a deep 28 cm (11 in) unheated frying pan, stirring to coat the garlic with the oil. Cook over medium heat for 2–3 minutes, swirling the pan regularly, until the garlic is fragrant and just starts to turn golden, and the anchovy melts into the oil.

3. Add the tomatoes, olives and capers, breaking up the tomatoes with a spoon if they are whole (or with your hands before adding, if you like). Simmer for 8–10 minutes, until slightly thickened. Taste and season with freshly ground black pepper, and salt if necessary.

4. Add the spaghetti and toss well to completely coat the pasta. Cover the pan and set aside for 1–2 minutes to allow the spaghetti to finish cooking and to absorb some of the sauce.

5. Divide between warmed serving bowls and serve.

Tomato vodka spaghetti

Creamy, tangy and a little spicy, here's a dish that feels indulgent and just retro enough to feel cool again. The vodka sharpens the tomatoes, the cream smooths everything out, and the result is glossy pink pasta you'll want to eat straight from the pan. Pairs well with... vodka!

Serves 2

200 g (7 oz) dried spaghetti
2 tablespoons extra virgin olive oil
2 garlic cloves, finely chopped
300 ml (10 fl oz) Italian tomato passata (pureed tomatoes)
60 ml (1/4 cup) cream (35% fat)
2 tablespoons vodka
large handful roughly chopped flat-leaf parsley

1. Cook the spaghetti in a large saucepan of boiling salted water for about 3 minutes less than specified on the packet, until slightly underdone and less than al dente. Drain.

2. Meanwhile, combine the olive oil and garlic, in a deep 28 cm (11 in) unheated frying pan, stirring to coat the garlic with the oil. Cook over medium–low heat for 30–60 seconds, stirring often, until the garlic is fragrant. Add the passata and bring to the boil over medium–high heat, then reduce the heat to medium–low and simmer for 5–6 minutes, until slightly thickened. Stir in the cream and bring back to the boil.

3. Add the spaghetti and vodka. Toss well, shaking the pan and stirring with a wooden spoon for about 1–2 minutes, until the pasta is al dente and well coated with the sauce. Taste and season with salt and freshly ground black pepper. Stir in the parsley.

4. Divide between warmed serving bowls or plates and serve immediately.

One-Pan

CENTONZE

Drunken spaghetti

A little butter, a good splash of red wine, and spaghetti that soaks up every drop of deep, inky flavour, this is pasta with a side of romance – dramatic colour, silky sauce, and just enough indulgence to feel like you're getting away with something.

Serves 2

2 tablespoons extra virgin olive oil
20 g (3/4 oz) salted butter
2 garlic cloves, finely chopped
250 ml (1 cup) decent-quality dry red wine
200 g (7 oz) dried spaghetti
handful roughly chopped flat-leaf parsley leaves
finely grated pecorino, to serve

1. Bring about 600 ml (20 fl oz) water to the boil, either in a kettle or covered saucepan.
2. Meanwhile, add the olive oil, butter, garlic and a few good pinches of salt to a deep 28 cm (11 in) frying pan. Place the pan over low heat and cook, stirring, for 1–2 minutes, until fragrant.
3. Add the red wine and 400 ml (13 1/2 fl oz) of the boiling water. Increase the heat to medium–high.
4. Add the spaghetti and, as it softens, push it into the pan and under the winey liquid with a wooden spoon. Cover for about a minute to bring to the boil, then remove the lid and stir with the wooden spoon to separate the pasta.
5. Leaving the lid off, simmer the spaghetti for about 5 minutes longer than specified on the packet, until the spaghetti is al dente, stirring regularly. As the end of the cooking time nears, shake the pan and stir with the wooden spoon, helping the oil and cooking liquid emulsify into a creamy sauce that coats the pasta. Add a little more boiling water if the mixture seems dry.
6. Stir in the parsley. Taste and season with salt and freshly ground black pepper.
7. Divide between warmed serving bowls, top generously with pecorino and serve immediately.

Lemon spaghetti

If sunshine could be twirled on a fork, it would look like this. Bright, zesty, glossy pasta that transports you straight to the Amalfi Coast – minus the airfare! Butter and parmesan keep it creamy, while lemon makes it sparkle. Ideal for summer nights, or for when your belly insists on pasta but also something a little lighter.

Serves 2

60 ml (1/4 cup) extra virgin olive oil
30 g (1 oz) butter
200 g (7 oz) dried spaghetti
zest and juice of 1 large lemon
20 g (1/4 cup) very finely grated parmesan
handful small basil leaves, to serve (optional)

1. Bring about 800 ml (27 fl oz) water to the boil, either in a kettle or covered saucepan.
2. Add the olive oil, butter, spaghetti, lemon zest and a few good pinches of salt to a deep 28 cm (11 in) frying pan. Place the pan over medium–high heat and carefully add 600 ml (20 fl oz) of the boiling water. As the spaghetti softens, push it into the pan and under the liquid with a wooden spoon. Cover for about a minute to bring to the boil, then remove the lid and stir with the wooden spoon to separate the pasta.
3. Leaving the lid off, simmer the spaghetti for about 3 minutes longer than specified on the packet, until the spaghetti is al dente, stirring regularly. As the end of the cooking time nears, add about half the lemon juice and shake the pan as you stir with the wooden spoon, helping the oil and cooking liquid emulsify into a creamy sauce that coats the pasta. Add a little more boiling water if the mixture seems dry.
4. Remove the pan from the heat and add the parmesan. Stir, shaking the pan, until melted and combined. Taste and season with salt and freshly ground black pepper, and more lemon juice, if necessary.
5. Divide between warmed serving bowls, scatter with basil, if you like, and serve.

ANNA
SALT
IODISED TABLE

Chicken stock & parmesan spaghetti

This is basically pasta cooked in its own sauce – creamy, silky, salty and so much more luxurious than its few ingredients suggest. The starch from the pasta water meets flavoursome chicken stock, parmesan melts in, and suddenly you have something velvety and comforting, all in the one pan. It's minimal effort, maximum payoff – the late-night pasta you didn't know you needed.

Serves 2

200 g (7 oz) dried spaghetti
30 g (1 oz) butter
60 ml (1/4 cup) extra virgin olive oil
800 ml (27 fl oz) good-quality chicken stock, approximately
40 g (1/2 cup) very finely grated parmesan, plus extra to serve
large handful small or roughly chopped flat-leaf parsley leaves (optional)

1. Add the spaghetti, butter, olive oil and 650 ml (22 fl oz) of the stock to a deep 28 cm (11 in) frying pan. Place the pan over high heat and bring to the boil. As the spaghetti softens, push it into the pan and under the liquid with a wooden spoon. Stir to separate the pasta.

2. Leaving the lid off, simmer the spaghetti for about 5 minutes longer than specified on the packet, until the spaghetti is al dente, stirring regularly. As the end of the cooking time nears, shake the pan and stir with the wooden spoon, helping the oil and stock emulsify into a creamy sauce that coats the pasta. Add a little more stock if the mixture seems dry.

3. Remove the pan from the heat and add the parmesan. Stir, shaking the pan, until melted and combined, then stir in the parsley, if using. Taste and season with salt and freshly ground black pepper.

4. Divide between warmed serving bowls, scatter with extra parmesan and serve immediately.

Sardine & cherry tomato spaghetti

Cherry tomatoes and sardines make a light, flavourful sauce when tossed together in the same pan as the spaghetti. Pine nuts add crunch, lemon brightens it up and spinach gives a fresh finish. It's the kind of pasta that feels both substantial and slightly Mediterranean, like you're on holiday, except it only took 20 minutes.

Serves 2

3 tablespoons pine nuts
2 tablespoons extra virgin olive oil, plus extra to serve
2 x 120 g (4½ oz) tins good-quality sardines in olive oil, bones removed if preferred
200 g (7 oz) dried spaghetti
250 g (9 oz) baby roma (plum) or cherry tomatoes
shredded zest and juice of 1 lemon
large handful baby spinach leaves

1. Bring about 800 ml (27 fl oz) water to the boil, either in a kettle or covered saucepan.

2. Meanwhile, toast the pine nuts in a dry frying pan over medium heat for 2–3 minutes, or until fragrant. Transfer the pine nuts to a plate and set aside.

3. Add the olive oil to the frying pan, along with 1 tablespoon of oil from the sardine tins. Add the spaghetti, tomatoes, lemon zest and a few good pinches of salt. Place the pan over medium–high heat and carefully add 600 ml (20 fl oz) of the boiling water. As the spaghetti softens, push it into the pan and under the liquid with a wooden spoon. Cover for about a minute to bring to the boil, then remove the lid and stir with the wooden spoon to separate the pasta.

4. Leaving the lid off, simmer the spaghetti for about 5 minutes longer than specified on the packet, until the spaghetti is al dente, stirring regularly. As the end of the cooking time nears, shake the pan and squish the tomatoes. Stir with the wooden spoon, helping the oil and cooking liquid emulsify into a creamy sauce that coats the pasta. Add a little more boiling water if the mixture seems dry.

5. Gently stir in the spinach, sardines and most of the pine nuts, retaining some chunks of sardine. Taste and season with salt, freshly ground black pepper and as much lemon juice as needed.

6. Divide between warmed serving bowls, scatter with the remaining pine nuts and serve immediately.

spaghetti

Tuna & lemon spaghetti

Tinned tuna finally finds the pasta dish it deserves: simple, briny and bright with lemon. Everything cooks together in one pan – spaghetti, capers, lemon zest, olive oil – then tuna and rocket are folded in at the end. Feta on top makes it a little salty, a little creamy and completely addictive. Midnight dinner, sorted.

Serves 2

60 ml (1/4 cup) extra virgin olive oil
200 g (7 oz) dried spaghetti
2 tablespoons capers, rinsed well if salted
finely grated zest and juice of 1 lemon
large handful roughly chopped rocket (arugula) or flat-leaf parsley leaves
185 g (6 1/2 oz) tin good-quality tuna chunks in olive oil, drained
crumbled feta, to serve (optional)

1. Bring about 800 ml (27 fl oz) water to the boil, either in a kettle or covered saucepan.
2. Add the olive oil, spaghetti, capers, lemon zest and a few good pinches of salt to a deep 28 cm (11 in) frying pan. Place the pan over medium–high heat and carefully add 600 ml (20 fl oz) of the boiling water. As the spaghetti softens, push it into the pan and under the liquid with a wooden spoon. Cover for about a minute to bring to the boil, then remove the lid and stir with the wooden spoon to separate the pasta.
3. Leaving the lid off, simmer the spaghetti for about 5 minutes longer than specified on the packet, until the spaghetti is al dente, stirring regularly. As the end of the cooking time nears, shake the pan and stir with the wooden spoon, helping the oil and cooking liquid emulsify into a creamy sauce that coats the pasta. Add a little more boiling water if the mixture seems dry.
4. Gently stir in the rocket and tuna, retaining some chunks of tuna. Taste and season with salt, freshly ground black pepper and as much lemon juice as needed.
5. Divide between warmed serving bowls, scatter with feta, if using, and serve.

Tip

For an extra flavour boost, replace some of the extra virgin olive oil with some of the olive oil from the tuna tin.

Smoked trout & creamy lemon spaghetti

This one-pan wonder tastes like it came straight out of a coastal holiday. Smoked trout, lemon and crème fraiche create a breezy sauce that's zesty, creamy and just the right amount of fancy.

Serves 2

2 tablespoons extra virgin olive oil
200 g (7 oz) dried spaghetti
shredded zest and juice of 1 lemon
80 ml (1/3 cup) dry white wine
large handful shredded kale leaves, baby spinach or sorrel leaves
125 g (1/2 cup) crème fraiche or sour cream
200 g (7 oz) flaked smoked trout

1. Bring about 800 ml (27 fl oz) water to the boil, either in a kettle or covered saucepan.

2. Add the olive oil, spaghetti, lemon zest, wine and a few good pinches of salt to a deep 28 cm (11 in) frying pan. Place the pan over medium–high heat and carefully add 600 ml (20 fl oz) of the boiling water. As the spaghetti softens, push it into the pan and under the liquid with a wooden spoon. Cover for about a minute to bring to the boil, then remove the lid and stir with the wooden spoon to separate the pasta.

3. Leaving the lid off, simmer the spaghetti for about the time specified on the packet, until the spaghetti is al dente, stirring regularly. After about 8 minutes, stir in the kale. As the end of the cooking time nears, stir in the crème fraiche. Shake the pan and stir with the wooden spoon, helping the cooking liquid emulsify into a creamy sauce that coats the pasta. Add a little more boiling water if the mixture seems dry.

4. Gently stir in the smoked trout, retaining some chunks and texture. Taste and season with salt, freshly ground black pepper and as much lemon juice as needed.

5. Divide between warmed serving bowls and serve immediately.

Assassins' spaghetti

This pasta doesn't whisper – it shouts. Cooked directly in spicy tomato sauce until the edges crisp and char, it's equal parts chewy and fiery. Think of it as arrabbiata with an edge, the kind of dish that feels a little rebellious and dramatic (in the best way). Ideally, use a heavy-based non-stick or cast-iron frying pan for this recipe.

Serves 2

60 ml (1/4 cup) extra virgin olive oil
2 garlic cloves, finely chopped
2 small red chillies, sliced, or 1–1½ teaspoons chilli flakes, plus extra to serve
250 ml (1 cup) Italian tomato passata (pureed tomatoes)
200 g (7 oz) dried spaghetti
stracciatella (see Tip), to serve

1. Bring about 650 ml (22 fl oz) water to the boil, either in a kettle or covered saucepan.
2. Meanwhile, add the olive oil, garlic and chilli to a deep 28 cm (11 in) frying pan. Place the pan over low heat and cook, stirring, for 1–2 minutes, until fragrant.
3. Add the passata, 500 ml (2 cups) of the boiling water and a few good pinches of salt. Increase the heat to medium–high. Stir well, then add the spaghetti and, as it softens, push it into the pan and under the tomato mixture with a wooden spoon.
4. Bring back to the boil. Without stirring, but jiggling the pan every now and then and shuffling the pasta with the wooden spoon, cook the spaghetti for about 5 minutes longer than specified on the packet, until the spaghetti is al dente, the liquid has reduced and thickened, and the underside of the pasta starts to brown. If the spaghetti is underdone at this point, add a little more boiling water and continue to cook until al dente.
5. Taste and season with salt and freshly ground black pepper. Stir, then cook without stirring for about 5 minutes, until the spaghetti makes a crackling sound, scorches and lightly chars in the pan. Using tongs, turn the pasta over so the browned bits are on top, then let the base scorch again.
6. Divide between warmed serving bowls, top with stracciatella and serve immediately.

Tip

Stracciatella is an Italian cheese made from fresh mozzarella that has been torn into fine strips and combined with cream. It is the delicious mixture that fills burrata. If you can't get hold of stracciatella you could use burrata or fresh mozzarella, torn into strips.

LEMON
SIMFRESH 4958
AUS

Fresh

BYRRH

LISTENTOTHEFLOWERSLISTENTOTHEFLOWERS

Caprese spaghetti

Like the classic salad, but more main event than side dish. Sweet tomatoes collapse into olive oil and garlic, slippery spaghetti soaks it all up, sweet peppery basil and mozzarella bring the freshness – and suddenly you're eating Italy in a bowl, no travel required.

Serves 2

200 g (7 oz) dried spaghetti
2 tablespoons extra virgin olive oil
250 g (9 oz) cherry tomatoes, cut in half
1 garlic clove, finely chopped
125 g (4½ oz) ball fresh buffalo mozzarella, sliced
handful basil leaves, to serve

1. Cook the spaghetti in a large saucepan of boiling salted water for about 3 minutes less than specified on the packet, until slightly underdone and less than al dente. Scoop out and reserve 250 ml (1 cup) of the pasta water and drain the pasta.

2. About 5 minutes before the spaghetti is ready, heat the olive oil and tomatoes in a deep 28 cm (11 in) frying pan over high heat for 3–4 minutes, swirling the pan regularly, until the tomatoes just start to collapse. Add the garlic and cook for a further minute or so, until the garlic is fragrant.

3. Add the spaghetti and 125 ml (½ cup) of the reserved pasta water, tossing well to completely coat the pasta. Add a little more pasta water if the mixture seems dry.

4. Cover the pan and set aside for 1–2 minutes to allow the spaghetti to finish cooking and to absorb a little of the tomatoey sauce. Taste and season with salt and freshly ground black pepper.

5. Divide between warmed serving bowls or plates, top with the mozzarella, scatter with the basil and serve.

Fried lemon, zucchini & ricotta spaghetti

Fresh and vibrant, this pasta combines golden discs of sauteed zucchini with creamy ricotta and the brightness of fried lemon slices. The result is a light, slightly tangy dish that feels both wholesome and uplifting. Parmesan ties it all together, but the real flex is squeezing in some extra lemon juice to suit yourself.

Serves 2

200 g (7 oz) dried spaghetti
1 lemon, plus extra lemon wedges to serve
60 ml (1/4 cup) extra virgin olive oil
3 small zucchini (courgettes), about 100 g (3 1/2 oz) each, sliced into 5 mm (1/4 in) thick coins
2 garlic cloves, finely chopped
125 g (1/2 cup) smooth ricotta (see Tip)
40 g (1/2 cup) very finely grated parmesan

1. Cook the spaghetti in a large saucepan of boiling salted water for about 3 minutes less than specified on the packet, until slightly underdone and less than al dente. Scoop out and reserve 375 ml (1 1/2 cups) of the pasta water and drain the pasta.

2. Meanwhile, finely zest the lemon and set the zest aside. Finely slice half the lemon and remove any seeds, then cut the slices into half-moons. Reserve the remaining half-lemon for the juice.

3. Combine the olive oil, zucchini, lemon slices and a good pinch of salt in a deep 28 cm (11 in) frying pan, stirring to coat the zucchini and lemon slices with the oil. Cook over medium–high heat for 5 minutes. Add the garlic and cook for a further 5–7 minutes, stirring occasionally, until the zucchini is very tender and lightly browned, and the garlic is fragrant.

4. Add 185 ml (3/4 cup) of the reserved pasta water, along with the lemon zest, ricotta and spaghetti. Toss well to coat the pasta, shaking the pan and stirring with a wooden spoon for a further 2–3 minutes, until the spaghetti is al dente and the sauce is smooth. Add a little more pasta water if the mixture seems dry.

5. Add the parmesan and stir, shaking the pan, until melted and combined. Taste and season with lemon juice, freshly ground black pepper and salt.

6. Divide between warmed serving bowls or plates and serve immediately, with extra lemon wedges.

Tip

Smooth, creamy ricotta that is high in moisture works best in this recipe – it will form a smooth sauce that coats the spaghetti with ease. If the ricotta is drained and firm, blitz it with a blender, adding a small amount of milk until smooth and dollop-able.

FIUGGI

Green olive, caper & lemon spaghetti

This is the pasta you make when you want bold flavours to wake you up, not lull you to sleep. Briny olives, salty capers and a good squeeze of lemon juice turn pantry staples into a dish that hits some serious flavour highs. Parmesan on top is optional, but highly encouraged – because pasta plus cheese is rarely a bad idea.

Serves 2

200 g (7 oz) dried spaghetti
60 ml (1/4 cup) extra virgin olive oil
1 garlic clove, finely chopped
60 g (1/2 cup) large pitted green olives, split lengthways
3 tablespoons capers, rinsed well if salted
1 lemon
parmesan, to serve (optional)

1. Cook the spaghetti in a large saucepan of boiling salted water for about 3 minutes less than specified on the packet, until slightly underdone and less than al dente. Do not drain.

2. About 3 minutes before the spaghetti is ready, combine the olive oil, garlic, olives and capers in a deep 28 cm (11 in) frying pan. Cook over medium heat for 1–2 minutes, until the garlic is fragrant, swirling the pan regularly.

3. Add 125 ml (1/2 cup) of the pasta water. Using tongs, add the spaghetti to the frying pan, straight from the saucepan. Finely grate the zest from the lemon into the pan, then squeeze in the juice from half the lemon.

4. Toss well to coat the pasta, shaking the pan and stirring with a wooden spoon for about 2 minutes, to finish cooking the spaghetti and to emulsify the oil, pasta water and lemon juice. Add a little more pasta water if the mixture seems dry. Taste and season with salt, white pepper and a little more lemon juice, if necessary.

5. Divide between warmed serving bowls. Grate some parmesan over the top, if you like, and serve immediately.

Tip

Slice 4 thin wedges from the second lemon half and use them to serve alongside the spaghetti.

PEP
Premium Black Pepper

Spaghetti with herby brown butter

Sometimes you don't want tomato, cream or even cheese – you just want butter. Browned until nutty, combined with spaghetti and flavoured with fresh herbs, this is minimalism at its finest.

Serves 2

200 g (7 oz) dried spaghetti
80 g (2¾ oz) butter
12 sage leaves
small handful oregano leaves
small handful parsley leaves
freshly grated parmesan, to serve (optional)

1. Cook the spaghetti in a large saucepan of boiling salted water for about 3 minutes less than specified on the packet, until slightly underdone and less than al dente. Scoop out and reserve 1 cup (250 ml) of the pasta water and drain the pasta.

2. About 5 minutes before the spaghetti is ready, melt the butter in a deep 28 cm (11 in) frying pan over medium heat for 2–3 minutes, until the butter foams, starts to turn golden brown and gives off a nutty aroma – be careful not to overcook it, or the milk solids may burn. Add the sage leaves and fry for 30 seconds more, or until the sage is fragrant.

3. Add 125 ml (½ cup) of the reserved pasta water, along with the spaghetti and most of the oregano and parsley. Toss well to coat the pasta, shaking the pan and stirring with a wooden spoon for a further 1–2 minutes, to finish cooking the spaghetti and to emulsify and thicken the sauce. Add a little more pasta water if the mixture seems dry. Taste and season with salt and freshly ground black pepper.

4. Divide between warmed serving bowls, scatter with the remaining herbs and serve with parmesan, if you like.

BYRRH
BYRRH

Dirty martini spaghetti

A martini you can twirl on a fork! Briny olives, sharp lemon and a splash of gin make this pasta taste like it just came from a cocktail bar. Parmesan softens the edges, and a toothpick of extra olives on top completes the vibe.

Serves 2

200 g (7 oz) dried spaghetti
3 tablespoons extra virgin olive oil
2 garlic cloves, finely sliced
1/2 lemon, finely sliced, then cut into half-moons
80 g (2 3/4 oz) large stuffed green olives, roughly chopped, plus 80 ml (1/3 cup) brine from the olives
2 tablespoons gin
40 g (1/2 cup) very finely grated parmesan, plus extra to serve

1. Cook the spaghetti in a large saucepan of boiling salted water for about 3 minutes less than specified on the packet, until slightly underdone and less than al dente. Scoop out and reserve 1 cup (250 ml) of the pasta water and drain the pasta.

2. Meanwhile, combine the olive oil, garlic and lemon slices in a deep 28 cm (11 in) unheated frying pan, stirring to coat the garlic and lemon slices with the oil. Cook over medium heat for 2–3 minutes, until the garlic is fragrant, swirling the pan regularly.

3. Add the olives and olive brine. Increase the heat to medium–high. Simmer for 1–2 minutes, until the liquid has reduced slightly.

4. Add the gin, 125 ml (1/2 cup) of the reserved pasta water and the spaghetti. Toss well to coat the pasta, shaking the pan and stirring with a wooden spoon for a further 1–2 minutes, to finish cooking the spaghetti and to emulsify the pan juices and pasta water. Add a little more pasta water if the mixture seems dry.

5. Remove the pan from the heat and add the parmesan. Stir, shaking the pan, until melted and combined. Taste and season with salt, if necessary.

6. Divide between warmed serving bowls, top with extra parmesan and serve immediately.

Spaghetti with peas & bacon

This is weeknight carbonara's cousin: buttery onions, salty bacon, sweet peas, parmesan. The kind of pasta that makes you feel nostalgic for something you probably didn't eat as a kid! A little smoky, a little creamy and a lot delicious – and the peas make you feel almost virtuous. Almost.

Serves 2

200 g (7 oz) dried spaghetti
20 g (3/4 oz) butter
1 small brown onion, chopped
2 slices rindless bacon, cut into thick strips
1 tablespoon extra virgin olive oil
140 g (1 cup) shelled fresh or frozen baby peas
40 g (1/2 cup) very finely grated parmesan, plus extra to serve

1. Cook the spaghetti in a large saucepan of boiling salted water for about 3 minutes less than specified on the packet, until slightly underdone and less than al dente. Scoop out and reserve 250 ml (1 cup) of the pasta water and drain the pasta.

2. Meanwhile, heat the butter, onion, bacon, olive oil and a good pinch of salt in a deep 28 cm (11 in) unheated frying pan, stirring to coat the onion and bacon with the oil. Cook over medium heat for 6–8 minutes, swirling the pan and stirring regularly, until the onion is tender and the bacon starts to brown. Add the peas and cook for a further 1–2 minutes, until tender. Lightly mash half the peas with the back of a spoon.

3. Add about 125 ml (1/2 cup) of the reserved pasta water and the spaghetti. Toss well to coat the pasta, shaking the pan and stirring with a wooden spoon for a further 1–2 minutes, to finish cooking the spaghetti and to emulsify the pan juices and pasta water. Add a little more pasta water if the mixture seems dry.

4. Remove the pan from the heat and add the parmesan. Stir, shaking the pan, until melted and combined. Taste and season generously with freshly ground black pepper, and salt if necessary.

5. Divide between warmed serving bowls and serve immediately, with extra parmesan.

Spring vegetable spaghetti

Fresh, green and light, this pasta makes perfect sense at midnight. Zucchini, asparagus and peas tumble together with lemon and feta, making this pasta feel like you've slipped into spring no matter the time of year. Add some pangrattato if you're craving some crunch, but honestly, it's bright and breezy enough on its own.

Serves 2

200 g (7 oz) dried spaghetti
60 ml (1/4 cup) extra virgin olive oil, plus extra to serve
2 small zucchini (courgettes), about 100 g (3 1/2 oz) each, sliced into 5 mm (1/4 in) thick coins
1 bunch asparagus, ends trimmed, sliced on the diagonal
85 g (2/3 cup) shelled fresh or frozen baby peas
crumbled feta, to serve
lemon wedges, to serve

1. Cook the spaghetti in a large saucepan of boiling salted water for about 3 minutes less than specified on the packet, until slightly underdone and less than al dente. Scoop out and reserve 250 ml (1 cup) of the pasta water and drain the pasta.

2. Meanwhile, heat the olive oil in a deep 28 cm (11 in) frying pan over medium heat. Add the zucchini and a good pinch of salt. Fry for 5–6 minutes, until tender and lightly browned, stirring occasionally. Add the asparagus and peas and cook for a further 2–3 minutes, until the asparagus is tender–crisp.

3. Add 185 ml (3/4 cup) of the reserved pasta water and the spaghetti. Toss well to coat the pasta, shaking the pan and stirring with a wooden spoon for a further 1–2 minutes, to finish cooking the spaghetti and to emulsify the pan juices and pasta water. Add a little more pasta water if the mixture seems dry. Taste and season with salt and freshly ground black pepper.

4. Divide between warmed serving bowls. Scatter with feta, drizzle with a little more olive oil, if you like, and serve immediately, with lemon wedges.

Optional extra

Add a quick crispy pangrattato! Before cooking the zucchini, add a good splash of olive oil to the frying pan, along with about 15 g (1/4 cup) panko breadcrumbs. Cook over medium–high heat, stirring constantly for 2–3 minutes, until golden, then transfer to a plate. Serve scattered over the spaghetti.

MASCHIO

Spaghetti with balsamic butter

This is what happens when brown butter and balsamic vinegar team up: nutty, tangy, and so good you'll want to slurp it from the pan. Toss in rocket to keep things lively and shower with parmesan if you're that kind of person (I am). The end result is rich, sharp and dangerously easy – the kind of pasta that feels like a secret handshake.

Serves 2

200 g (7 oz) dried spaghetti
1 tablespoon extra virgin olive oil
80 g (2¾ oz) butter
1 garlic clove, finely chopped
2 tablespoons good-quality aged balsamic vinegar, plus extra to serve
large handful rocket (arugula) leaves
parmesan or pecorino romano, to serve (optional)

1. Cook the spaghetti in a large saucepan of boiling salted water for about 3 minutes less than specified on the packet, until slightly underdone and less than al dente. Scoop out and reserve 250 ml (1 cup) of the pasta water and drain the pasta.

2. About 5 minutes before the spaghetti is ready, heat the olive oil, butter and garlic in a deep 28 cm (11 in) frying pan. Cook over medium heat for 3–4 minutes, until the garlic is fragrant, and the butter starts to turn golden brown and gives off a nutty aroma – be careful not to overcook the butter, or the milk solids may burn.

3. Stir in the balsamic vinegar and cook for 1 minute, then add 125 ml (½ cup) of the reserved pasta water, along with the spaghetti and rocket. Toss well to coat the pasta, shaking the pan and stirring with a wooden spoon for a further 1–2 minutes, to finish cooking the spaghetti and to emulsify the sauce. Add a little more pasta water if the mixture seems dry. Taste and season with salt and freshly ground black pepper.

4. Divide between warmed serving bowls and serve with extra balsamic vinegar, and a fresh grating of cheese, if you like.

Walnut & mascarpone spaghetti

Toasted walnuts and mascarpone create a sauce that's creamy and nutty, brightened with a little lemon. Finished with sage, this is a pasta that feels a little dressed up, but is sneakily easy, making it a magic midnight meal.

Serves 2

200 g (7 oz) dried spaghetti
50 g (1/2 cup) walnuts, roughly chopped
1 tablespoon extra virgin olive oil
2 garlic cloves, finely sliced
4 teaspoons shredded sage leaves, plus extra to serve
125 g (4 1/2 oz) mascarpone
juice of 1/2 lemon, plus extra to taste

1. Cook the spaghetti in a large saucepan of boiling salted water for about 3 minutes less than specified on the packet, until slightly underdone and less than al dente. Scoop out and reserve 250 ml (1 cup) of the pasta water and drain the pasta.

2. Meanwhile, add the walnuts to a deep 28 cm (11 in) unheated dry frying pan over medium heat. Toast the walnuts, stirring occasionally, for 4–5 minutes, until fragrant and just starting to colour. Transfer to a plate and set aside.

3. Add the olive oil, garlic and sage to the frying pan. Cook, stirring, for 1–2 minutes, until the garlic is fragrant.

4. Add 80 ml (1/3 cup) of the reserved pasta water and the mascarpone. Stir until combined, bring to the boil, then reduce the heat to a simmer.

5. Add the spaghetti and most of the walnuts. Toss well to coat the pasta, shaking the pan and stirring with a wooden spoon for 2–3 minutes, until the pasta is al dente and the sauce has thickened and coats the pasta.

6. Squeeze in the lemon juice. Taste and season with salt, freshly ground black pepper and a little more lemon juice, if necessary. Add a little more pasta water if the sauce needs thinning.

7. Divide between warmed serving bowls or plates, scatter the remaining walnuts and extra sage over the top and serve.

Bold

EXTRA VIRGIN OLIVE OIL
RISERVA
CENTON
CASTELVETRANO
OLIVE VERDI SCHIACCIATE

Delicius
Canale di Sicilia

Anchovy & cherry tomato spaghetti

Sweet cherry tomatoes, briny olives and dreamy anchovies that melt into oil like butter – this is peak umami. This spaghetti is salty, juicy and just messy enough to feel like you made something special without actually trying that hard. The trick is splurging on good anchovies; they're the unsung heroes here.

Serves 2

200 g (7 oz) dried spaghetti
3 tablespoons extra virgin olive oil
2 garlic cloves, finely sliced
47 g (1½ oz) tin good-quality anchovy fillets in olive oil, drained and chopped
250 g (9 oz) cherry tomatoes, cut in half
80 g (½ cup) pitted green olives, roughly chopped
handful roughly chopped flat-leaf parsley leaves, to serve (optional)

1. Cook the spaghetti in a large saucepan of boiling salted water for about 3 minutes less than specified on the packet, until slightly underdone and less than al dente. Scoop out and reserve 250 ml (1 cup) of the pasta water and drain the pasta.

2. About 5 minutes before the spaghetti is ready, combine the olive oil, garlic, anchovy and tomatoes in a deep 28 cm (11 in) unheated frying pan, stirring to coat the garlic, anchovy and tomatoes with the oil. Cook over medium heat for 4–5 minutes, swirling the pan regularly, until the garlic is fragrant, the anchovy melts into the oil and the tomatoes just start to collapse.

3. Add the spaghetti, olives and 125 ml (½ cup) of the reserved pasta water. Toss well to coat the pasta, shaking the pan and stirring with a wooden spoon to emulsify the pan juices and pasta water.

4. Cover the pan and set aside for 1–2 minutes to allow the spaghetti to finish cooking and to absorb a little of the tomatoey anchovy sauce. Taste and season with freshly ground black pepper and salt, if necessary.

5. Divide between warmed serving bowls or plates and serve, scattered with parsley, if you like.

Crispy chilli oil & spring onion spaghetti

This is what happens when spaghetti crashes a Chinese takeout night. Spring onions dance with crispy chilli oil and soy sauce, and the spaghetti soaks it all up like a sponge. Parmesan sneaks in for creaminess (don't question it, it works). Fiery, salty, a little funky – it's the kind of bowl you'll want to eat standing at the kitchen counter, extra chilli oil on the side.

Serves 2

200 g (7 oz) dried spaghetti
1 tablespoon peanut oil
3 spring onions (scallions), finely sliced, plus extra to serve
2 tablespoons crispy chilli oil (see Tip), plus extra to serve
1 tablespoon good-quality light soy sauce, plus extra to serve
40 g (1/2 cup) very finely grated parmesan

1. Cook the spaghetti in a large saucepan of boiling salted water for about 3 minutes less than specified on the packet, until slightly underdone and less than al dente. Scoop out and reserve 250 ml (1 cup) of the pasta water and drain the pasta.

2. About 5 minutes before the spaghetti is ready, combine the peanut oil and spring onion in a deep 28 cm (11 in) frying pan. Cook over medium heat for 2–3 minutes, until fragrant, swirling the pan regularly.

3. Add 125 ml (1/2 cup) of the reserved pasta water, along with the spaghetti, crispy chilli oil and soy sauce. Toss well to coat the pasta, shaking the pan and stirring with a wooden spoon for a further 1–2 minutes, to finish cooking the spaghetti and to emulsify the pan juices and pasta water. Add a little more pasta water if the mixture seems dry.

4. Remove the pan from the heat and add the parmesan. Stir, shaking the pan, until melted and combined. Taste and season with extra soy sauce, if necessary.

5. Divide between warmed serving bowls or plates. Top with extra spring onion and crispy chilli oil. Serve immediately, with more soy sauce to the side.

Tip

Crispy chilli oil – also known as chilli crisp – is a spicy condiment comprising a bright deep red oil infused with dried chillies, Sichuan peppercorns and spices. The crispy part comes from fried garlic, shallots or onion, and sometimes peanuts. It is available from Asian grocery stores and larger supermarkets.

Spanish prawn & chorizo spaghetti

This is the kind of pasta that knows how to party – smoky chorizo, sweet juicy prawns, tangy cherry tomatoes and creamy chickpeas all jostling for attention in one pan. Big, bold Spanish flavours with minimal fuss.

Serves 2

200 g (7 oz) dried spaghetti
1 teaspoon extra virgin olive oil, plus extra to serve
120 g (4½ oz) Spanish-style cured chorizo sausage, finely sliced
200 g (7 oz) peeled raw prawns (shrimp) with tails intact
250 g (9 oz) cherry tomatoes, cut in half
1 teaspoon smoked paprika
400 g (14 oz) tin chickpeas, drained

1. Cook the spaghetti in a large saucepan of boiling salted water for about 3 minutes less than specified on the packet, until slightly underdone and less than al dente. Scoop out and reserve 250 ml (1 cup) of the pasta water and drain the pasta.

2. Meanwhile, combine the olive oil and chorizo in a deep 28 cm (11 in) unheated frying pan, stirring to coat the chorizo with the oil. Cook over medium heat for 2–3 minutes, swirling the pan regularly, until the chorizo begins to release its oil and become translucent.

3. Increase the heat to medium–high. Add the prawns and cook for 3–4 minutes, stirring occasionally, until the prawns are just cooked through, with a little browning. Transfer the chorizo and prawns to a plate using a slotted spoon, cover to keep warm and set aside.

4. Add the tomatoes and paprika to the pan and cook, stirring, for a further 3–4 minutes, until the tomatoes collapse.

5. Add 125 ml (½ cup) of the reserved pasta water and the spaghetti to the pan, along with the chorizo, prawns and chickpeas. Toss well to coat the pasta, shaking the pan and stirring with a wooden spoon for a further 1–2 minutes, to finish cooking the spaghetti and to emulsify the pan juices and pasta water. Add a little more pasta water if the mixture seems dry.

6. Taste and season with salt and freshly ground black pepper, if necessary.

7. Divide between warmed serving bowls. Drizzle with a little more olive oil and serve immediately.

Baby broccoli, anchovy & chilli spaghetti

This dish is living proof that greens at midnight can feel wickedly indulgent, not virtuous. The anchovies melt into olive oil, garlic and chilli, making the kind of sauce you could eat with bread alone. Baby broccoli adds colour and crunch to the pasta, then it's all topped with a snowy drift of parmesan. For an extra anchovy punch, use some of the anchovy oil from the tin in place of the olive oil.

Serves 2

200 g (7 oz) dried spaghetti
2 tablespoons extra virgin olive oil, plus extra to serve
2 garlic cloves, finely chopped
3 good-quality anchovy fillets in olive oil, drained and chopped
1/2–1 teaspoon chilli flakes
1 bunch baby broccoli, stalks sliced, heads cut into florets
freshly grated parmesan, to serve

1. Cook the spaghetti in a large saucepan of boiling salted water for about 3 minutes less than specified on the packet, until slightly underdone and less than al dente. Scoop out and reserve 250 ml (1 cup) of the pasta water and drain the pasta.

2. Meanwhile, combine the olive oil, garlic, anchovy and chilli flakes in a deep 28 cm (11 in) unheated frying pan, stirring to coat the anchovy, garlic and chilli with the oil. Cook over medium heat for 2–3 minutes, swirling the pan regularly, until the garlic is fragrant and the anchovy melts into the oil.

3. Add the broccoli and cook for 3–4 minutes, until bright green and tender-crisp.

4. Add 80 ml (1/3 cup) of the reserved pasta water and the spaghetti. Toss well to coat the pasta, shaking the pan and stirring with a wooden spoon for a further 1–2 minutes, to finish cooking the spaghetti and to emulsify the pan juices and pasta water. Add a little more pasta water if the mixture seems dry. Taste and season with freshly ground black pepper, and salt, if necessary.

5. Divide between warmed serving bowls, drizzle with extra olive oil, top generously with parmesan and serve immediately.

Sichuan chilli pork spaghetti

This pasta doesn't tiptoe around flavour – it kicks the door in. Pork gets browned and tossed with chilli sauce, sesame paste, chilli oil and black vinegar for a deep, spicy Sichuan hit. Peanuts add crunch and texture, while the spaghetti soaks up all the delicious flavours.

Serves 2

200 g (7 oz) dried spaghetti
1 tablespoon chilli oil, plus extra to serve
250 g (9 oz) minced (ground) pork
4 tablespoons toban djan chilli sauce or doubanjiang chilli bean paste
2 tablespoons Chinese sesame paste (or tahini in a pinch)
2 teaspoons black vinegar, or to taste
handful of roasted peanuts, roughly chopped, to serve

1. Cook the spaghetti in a large saucepan of boiling salted water for about 3 minutes less than specified on the packet, until slightly underdone and less than al dente. Scoop out and reserve 375 ml (1½ cups) of the pasta water and drain the pasta.

2. Meanwhile, heat the chilli oil in a deep 28 cm (11 in) frying pan over medium–high heat. Crumble in the pork and cook, breaking up the pork and stirring occasionally, for 5–7 minutes, until well browned. Add 3 tablespoons of the chilli sauce or bean paste, stir well and cook for a further 2 minutes, or until fragrant. Transfer to a warmed plate and cover to keep warm.

3. Add 250 ml (1 cup) of the reserved pasta water to the pan, along with the sesame paste and the remaining 1 tablespoon of chilli sauce or bean paste. Stir well.

4. Add the spaghetti to the pan. Toss well to coat the pasta, shaking the pan and stirring with a wooden spoon for a further 1–2 minutes to finish cooking the spaghetti and to emulsify the pan juices and pasta water. Add a little more pasta water if the mixture seems dry.

5. Taste and season with the black vinegar.

6. Divide between warmed serving bowls, top with the chilli pork, scatter with peanuts and serve.

Tip

Chilli oil, toban djan chilli sauce, doubanjiang chilli bean paste and Chinese sesame paste are all available at Asian grocery stores.

SANGIOVESE

Garlic prawns & nduja spaghetti

Think of this as prawn pasta with the volume turned right up. Garlicky prawns flirt with spicy nduja, which melts into little fiery pockets of flavour. Parsley lightens the mood, but really it's all about the prawns and that chilli kick.

Serves 2

200 g (7 oz) dried spaghetti
2 tablespoons extra virgin olive oil
100 g (3½ oz) nduja (see Tip), crumbled
30 g (1 oz) butter
3 garlic cloves, finely chopped
200 g (7 oz) peeled raw prawns (shrimp), cut into 1.5 cm (½ in) pieces
large handful chopped flat-leaf parsley, plus extra to serve

1. Cook the spaghetti in a large saucepan of boiling salted water for about 3 minutes less than specified on the packet, until slightly underdone and less than al dente. Scoop out and reserve 250 ml (1 cup) of the pasta water and drain the pasta.

2. Meanwhile, combine 1 teaspoon of the olive oil and the nduja in a deep 28 cm (11 in) unheated frying pan, stirring gently to coat the nduja with the oil. Cook over medium heat for 2–3 minutes, swirling the pan regularly and carefully to keep the nduja in little nubs, until the nduja begins to release its oil. Using a slotted spoon, carefully transfer the nduja to a plate and set aside.

3. Add the remaining oil, butter and garlic to the pan and cook, stirring, for 1–2 minutes, until fragrant. Add the chopped prawns and cook, stirring until the prawns are opaque, lightly browned and just cooked through.

4. Add 125 ml (½ cup) of the reserved pasta water, along with the spaghetti and parsley. Toss well to coat the pasta, shaking the pan and stirring with a wooden spoon for a further 1–2 minutes, to finish cooking the spaghetti and to emulsify the pan juices and pasta water. Add a little more pasta water if the mixture seems dry. Fold the nduja through.

5. Taste and season with salt and freshly ground black pepper, if necessary.

6. Divide between warmed serving bowls or plates. Scatter with extra parsley and serve immediately.

Tip

Nduja is a spicy soft, spreadable pork sausage originating from Calabria in southern Italy. You can buy it from good delicatessens.

Spaghetti with chipotle meatballs

Classic meatballs, but with a smoky, spicy twist. Chipotle brings the heat, spinach softens it, and creamy cubes of avocado cool things down. It's spaghetti and meatballs with a little swagger.

Serves 2

200 g (7 oz) dried spaghetti
1 tablespoon extra virgin olive oil
250 g (9 oz) pork and oregano sausages
400 g (14 oz) tin crushed tomatoes
2 tablespoons chopped chipotle chillies in adobo sauce
2 large handfuls baby spinach leaves
1/2 small avocado, cut into cubes

1. Cook the spaghetti in a large saucepan of boiling salted water for about 3 minutes less than specified on the packet, until slightly underdone and less than al dente. Drain.

2. Meanwhile, heat the olive oil in a deep 28 cm (11 in) frying pan over medium–high heat. Squeeze the sausage meat out of the skins in small ball shapes and add to the pan. Shake the pan to coat the meatballs with the oil. Cook for 3–5 minutes, shaking the pan regularly, until the meatballs are well browned, but not cooked through.

3. Add the tomatoes, chopped chipotles and adobo sauce. Bring to the boil, then reduce the heat and simmer for about 5 minutes, until the sauce thickens slightly. Add the spinach and spaghetti and stir until combined. Taste and season with salt, freshly ground black pepper and a little sugar if necessary.

4. Remove from the heat, cover and set aside for 2 minutes to allow the spaghetti to finish cooking and to absorb some of the sauce.

5. Divide between warmed serving bowls, top with the avocado and serve immediately.

Gochujang chicken spaghetti

Here, chicken and spaghetti are coated in a sauce of gochujang, sesame and soy for a dish that's gently spicy and deeply satisfying. A side of kimchi adds brightness and crunch to balance the richness.

Serves 2

200 g (7 oz) dried spaghetti
250 g (9 oz) boneless, skinless chicken thighs, cut into 1.5 cm (1/2 in) chunks
2 teaspoons soy sauce
2 teaspoons sesame oil, plus extra to serve
2 tablespoons gochujang (Korean chilli paste)
1 tablespoon vegetable oil
kimchi, to serve

1. Cook the spaghetti in a large saucepan of boiling salted water for about 3 minutes less than specified on the packet, until slightly underdone and less than al dente. Scoop out and reserve 250 ml (1 cup) of the pasta water and drain the pasta.
2. Meanwhile, mix the chicken in a bowl with the soy sauce, sesame oil and 1 tablespoon of the gochujang until well combined.
3. Heat the vegetable oil in a deep 28 cm (11 in) frying pan over medium–high heat. Add the chicken and cook for 4–6 minutes, stirring occasionally, until the chicken is lightly charred and just cooked through.
4. Reduce the heat to medium and add 125 ml (1/2 cup) of the reserved pasta water, along with the spaghetti and the remaining 1 tablespoon of gochujang. Toss well to combine and coat the pasta, shaking the pan and stirring with a wooden spoon for a further 1–2 minutes, to finish cooking the spaghetti and to emulsify the pan juices and pasta water. Add a little more pasta water if the mixture seems dry.
5. Taste and season with a little more sesame oil if necessary.
6. Divide between warmed serving bowls, top with kimchi and serve immediately.

Optional extras

Add a scattering of toasted sesame seeds.

Spaghetti with chorizo & crispy croutons

Spicy chorizo twirls with sweet roasted peppers in this Spanish flamenco of a spaghetti dish, swirled with spinach and topped with golden, crunchy croutons. A sassy splash of vinegar is all that's needed for a simple but vibrant finish.

Serves 2

200 g (7 oz) dried spaghetti
3 tablespoons extra virgin olive oil, plus extra to serve
2 thick slices stale sourdough bread, torn into 1 cm (1/2 in) chunks
120 g (4 1/2 oz) Spanish-style cured chorizo sausage, crumbled or roughly chopped
100 g (3 1/2 oz) roasted red bell pepper (capsicum), roughly chopped
2 large handfuls baby spinach leaves
Spanish sherry vinegar, to taste

1. Cook the spaghetti in a large saucepan of boiling salted water for about 3 minutes less than specified on the packet, until slightly underdone and less than al dente. Scoop out and reserve 250 ml (1 cup) of the pasta water and drain the pasta.

2. Meanwhile, heat 2 tablespoons of the olive oil in a deep 28 cm (11 in) frying pan over medium–high heat. Add the sourdough pieces and a good pinch of salt. Cook for 3–5 minutes, swirling the pan and stirring regularly, until the bread turns golden. Transfer to a plate and set aside to cool and crisp up.

3. Reduce the heat to medium and add the chorizo and remaining 1 tablespoon of oil to the pan. Cook, stirring occasionally, for 2–3 minutes, until the fat renders from the chorizo and the sausage starts to brown. Stir in the chopped red pepper.

4. Add 125 ml (1/2 cup) of the reserved pasta water, along with the spinach and spaghetti. Toss well to coat the pasta, shaking the pan and stirring with a wooden spoon for a further 1–2 minutes, to finish cooking the spaghetti and to emulsify the pan juices and pasta water. Add a little more pasta water if the mixture seems dry.

5. Taste and season with freshly ground black pepper, salt and sherry vinegar.

6. Divide between warmed serving bowls, scatter the crispy croutons over the top and serve immediately.

Sriracha hot sauce spaghetti

Turn up the heat! This spaghetti is fiery, punchy and unapologetically simple – garlic, spring onion, a generous splash of sriracha, and plenty of parmesan to keep things creamy. A quick dish for when you want comfort with a little spice.

Serves 2

200 g (7 oz) dried spaghetti
3 tablespoons peanut oil
2 spring onions (scallions), finely sliced, plus extra to serve
2 garlic cloves, finely chopped
3 tablespoons sriracha hot sauce, or to taste
40 g (1/2 cup) very finely grated parmesan
lime wedges, to serve (optional)

1. Cook the spaghetti in a large saucepan of boiling salted water for about 3 minutes less than specified on the packet, until slightly underdone and less than al dente. Scoop out and reserve 250 ml (1 cup) of the pasta water and drain the pasta.

2. About 5 minutes before the spaghetti is ready, combine the peanut oil, spring onion and garlic in a deep 28 cm (11 in) frying pan. Cook over low heat for 1–2 minutes, until fragrant, swirling the pan regularly.

3. Add the sriracha, 125 ml (1/2 cup) of the reserved pasta water and the spaghetti. Toss well to coat the pasta, shaking the pan and stirring with a wooden spoon for a further 1–2 minutes, to finish cooking the spaghetti and to emulsify the pan juices and pasta water. Add a little more pasta water if the mixture seems dry.

4. Remove the pan from the heat and add the parmesan. Stir, shaking the pan, until melted and combined.

5. Divide between warmed serving bowls or plates and serve immediately, with the extra spring onion scattered over and lime wedges, if you like.

Street corn spaghetti

Inspired by grilled Mexican street corn, this pasta is tangy, cheesy and full of crunch. Sweet charred corn, pickled jalapenos, feta and fresh coriander all dance together in a bowl that's both fun and fresh.

Serves 2

200 g (7 oz) dried spaghetti
3 tablespoons vegetable oil
1 corn cob, kernels removed, or 150 g (1 cup) frozen corn kernels
2 garlic cloves, finely chopped
1 tablespoon sliced pickled jalapeno chillies, roughly chopped, plus 3 tablespoons of the pickled jalapeno brine, and extra sliced jalapeno to serve
large handful coriander (cilantro), stems chopped, leaves picked
40 g (1/4 cup) crumbled feta, plus extra to serve

1. Cook the spaghetti in a large saucepan of boiling salted water for about 3 minutes less than specified on the packet, until slightly underdone and less than al dente. Scoop out and reserve 250 ml (1 cup) of the pasta water and drain the pasta.

2. Meanwhile, heat the vegetable oil in a deep 28 cm (11 in) frying pan over high heat. Add the corn kernels and cook for 4–5 minutes, stirring occasionally, until the corn is slightly charred. Reduce the heat to medium and add the garlic, chopped jalapeno and coriander stems. Cook for 1–2 minutes, stirring, until the garlic is fragrant.

3. Add the jalapeno brine, 125 ml (1/2 cup) of the reserved pasta water and the spaghetti. Toss well to coat the pasta, shaking the pan and stirring with a wooden spoon for a further 1–2 minutes, to finish cooking the spaghetti and to emulsify the pan juices and pasta water. Add a little more pasta water if the mixture seems dry.

4. Toss in the coriander leaves and feta. Taste and season with salt, if necessary.

5. Divide between warmed serving bowls and serve immediately, scattered with extra feta and jalapeno slices.

Bulgogi, spinach & sesame spaghetti

If Korean bulgogi and Italian pasta had a dinner date, this would be the result: thin slices of deliciously caramelised beef, tangled through slippery spaghetti with a slick of sesame oil and baby spinach. Sweet, savoury and a little glossy, it's a proper crowd-pleaser... and simply deluxe when dining solo.

Serves 2

200 g (7 oz) dried spaghetti
250 g (9 oz) beef sirloin (porterhouse) or rump steak, very finely sliced
3 tablespoons bulgogi marinade sauce
2 tablespoons vegetable oil
2 large handfuls baby spinach leaves
2 teaspoons toasted sesame oil, plus extra to taste
toasted sesame seeds, to serve

1. Cook the spaghetti in a large saucepan of boiling salted water for about 3 minutes less than specified on the packet, until slightly underdone and less than al dente. Scoop out and reserve 375 ml (1½ cups) of the pasta water and drain the pasta.

2. Meanwhile, in a small bowl, combine the beef and 2 tablespoons of the bulgogi marinade mixing well.

3. Heat the vegetable oil in a deep 28 cm (11 in) frying pan over high heat. Add half the beef in a single layer and allow to brown well for 1–2 minutes before turning and cooking for a further minute or so, until slightly charred and barely cooked through. Transfer to a warmed plate, cover to keep warm and set aside. Repeat with the remaining beef.

4. Add 185 ml (¾ cup) of the reserved pasta water to the pan. Add the spinach, spaghetti, sesame oil and remaining 1 tablespoon of bulgogi marinade. Toss well to coat the pasta, shaking the pan and stirring with a wooden spoon for a further 1–2 minutes, to finish cooking the spaghetti and to emulsify the pan juices and pasta water. Add a little more pasta water if the mixture seems dry.

5. Return the beef to the pan. Taste and season with salt and freshly ground black pepper, and extra sesame oil if necessary.

6. Divide between warmed serving bowls. Scatter with sesame seeds and serve immediately.

Prawns & crispy chilli oil spaghetti

This pasta doesn't whisper – it crackles. Juicy prawns, fiery crispy chilli oil, garlicky chives and sweet, chewy savoury lap cheong make for a bowl that's bold, punchy… and impossible to put down.

Serves 2

200 g (7 oz) dried spaghetti
1 teaspoon peanut oil
60 g lap cheong (Chinese preserved sausage), finely sliced
200 g (7 oz) peeled raw prawns (shrimp) with tails intact, butterflied
2 tablespoons crispy chilli oil (see Tip below, and on page 77), plus extra to serve
2 large handfuls garlic chives, cut into 3 cm (1¼ in) lengths
lemon wedges, to serve

1. Cook the spaghetti in a large saucepan of boiling salted water for about 3 minutes less than specified on the packet, until slightly underdone and less than al dente. Scoop out and reserve 250 ml (1 cup) of the pasta water and drain the pasta.

2. Meanwhile, combine the peanut oil and lap cheong in a deep 28 cm (11 in) unheated frying pan, stirring to coat the sausage with the oil. Cook over medium heat for 2–3 minutes, swirling the pan regularly, until the sausage begins to release its oil and becomes translucent. Transfer the sausage to a plate using a slotted spoon and set aside.

3. Increase the heat to medium–high and add the prawns to the pan. Cook for 3–4 minutes, until the prawns are just cooked through, with a little browning. Return the sausage to the pan and add the crispy chilli oil and garlic chives. Cook, stirring, for a further 1–2 minutes, until the ingredients are well combined and the chives are wilted.

4. Add 185 ml (¾ cup) of the reserved pasta water and the spaghetti. Toss well to coat the pasta, shaking the pan and stirring with a wooden spoon for a further 1–2 minutes, to finish cooking the spaghetti and to emulsify the pan juices and pasta water. Add a little more pasta water if the mixture seems dry.

5. Taste and season with a little more crispy chilli oil, if necessary.

6. Divide between warmed serving bowls. Top with more crispy chilli oil and serve immediately, with lemon wedges.

Tip

Before adding the crispy chilli oil to the pan, give it a good stir to combine the crispy chilli bits and the spicy oil, so some of each ends up in the dish.

Cosy

BYRRH
BYRRH
BYRRH
FOOD
Paola
Bacchia

Creamy mushroom & thyme spaghetti

Mushrooms and cream were made for late-night cooking: fast, forgiving and richer than they have any right to be at this hour. Toss in some garlic, thyme and parmesan and you're rewarded with something silky yet earthy that clings beautifully to pasta. It's comfort food that feels slightly grown-up – like mac and cheese's French cousin.

Serves 2

200 g (7 oz) dried spaghetti
2 tablespoons extra virgin olive oil
200 g (7 oz) Swiss brown mushrooms, finely sliced
1 garlic clove, finely chopped
1 teaspoon thyme leaves
125 g (1/2 cup) sour cream or cream (35% fat)
25 g (1/3 cup) finely grated parmesan, plus extra to serve

1. Cook the spaghetti in a large saucepan of boiling salted water for about 3 minutes less than specified on the packet, until slightly underdone and less than al dente. Scoop out and reserve 250 ml (1 cup) of the pasta water and drain the pasta.

2. Meanwhile, heat the olive oil in a deep 28 cm (11 in) frying pan over medium–high heat. Add the mushrooms and a good pinch of salt and cook, stirring occasionally, for 4–5 minutes, until the mushrooms are lightly browned and release their juices. Add the garlic and thyme and cook, stirring, for 1–2 minutes, until the garlic is fragrant.

3. Add 125 ml (1/2 cup) of the reserved pasta water and the cream. Bring to the boil, then reduce the heat to a simmer.

4. Add the spaghetti and parmesan and stir with a wooden spoon until the cheese melts into the sauce. Simmer for 3–5 minutes, stirring and shaking the pan, until the sauce is slightly thickened and coats the pasta. Taste and season with salt and freshly ground black pepper.

5. Divide between warmed serving bowls, grate some extra parmesan over the top and serve.

Japanese soy-buttered spaghetti

Butter and soy sauce combine in this simple but flavourful spaghetti, tossed with pan-fried shiitake mushrooms and edamame. Finished with a touch of shichimi togarashi or sesame seeds, it's a comforting bowl with a Japanese accent.

Serves 2

200 g (7 oz) dried spaghetti
50 g (1¾ oz) butter, plus extra to serve
1 tablespoon peanut oil
50 g (1¾ oz) shiitake mushrooms, finely sliced
150 g (1 cup) podded frozen edamame
1 tablespoon good-quality Japanese soy sauce, plus extra to serve
shichimi togarashi or roasted black sesame seeds, to serve

1. Cook the spaghetti in a large saucepan of boiling salted water for about 3 minutes less than specified on the packet, until slightly underdone and less than al dente. Scoop out and reserve 250 ml (1 cup) of the pasta water and drain the pasta.
2. About 5 minutes before the spaghetti is ready, melt the butter and peanut oil in a deep 28 cm (11 in) frying pan over medium heat. When the butter is foaming, add the mushrooms and edamame. Cook, stirring, for 3–4 minutes, until the mushrooms are tender and fragrant.
3. Add 125 ml (½ cup) of the reserved pasta water, along with the spaghetti and soy sauce. Toss well to coat the pasta, shaking the pan and stirring with a wooden spoon for a further 1–2 minutes, to finish cooking the spaghetti and to emulsify the pan juices and pasta water. Add a little more pasta water if the mixture seems dry.
4. Divide between warmed serving bowls. Top each bowl with a slice of cold butter and a sprinkle of shichimi togarashi or sesame seeds. Serve immediately, with extra soy sauce to the side.

SHICHIMI
TOGARASHI

Cream cheese & everything bagel spaghetti

This one's giving 'bagel shop at midnight but make it pasta' vibes. Cream cheese melts into a glossy sauce, spiked with everything bagel seasoning and singing with lemon. Rocket keeps it fresh and peppery, while crushed bagel crisps (or pretzels, if that's what's lurking in the cupboard) add crunch. It's playful, comforting and slightly chaotic – in other words, perfect.

Serves 2

200 g (7 oz) dried spaghetti
80 g (1/3 cup) spreadable cream cheese
1 tablespoon everything bagel seasoning, plus extra to serve
finely grated zest and juice of 1 lemon
large handful rocket (arugula) leaves, roughly chopped
crushed bagel crackers or pretzels, to serve

1. Cook the spaghetti in a large saucepan of boiling salted water for about 3 minutes less than specified on the packet, until slightly underdone and less than al dente. Scoop out and reserve 250 ml (1 cup) of the pasta water and drain the pasta.

2. About 5 minutes before the spaghetti is ready, using a heatproof measuring jug, scoop 185 ml (3/4 cup) pasta water from the cooking spaghetti and pour it into a deep 28 cm (11 in) frying pan. Place over medium heat and add the cream cheese, bagel seasoning and lemon zest, stirring well. Bring to the boil, then reduce the heat to a simmer.

3. Add the spaghetti and rocket to the pan. Stir with a wooden spoon for a further 1–2 minutes, to finish cooking the spaghetti, shaking the pan until the sauce coats the pasta. Add a little more pasta water to thin the sauce if required. Taste and season with the lemon juice, salt and freshly ground black pepper.

4. Divide between warmed serving bowls. Scatter some bagel crumbs over the top, sprinkle with a little more bagel seasoning and serve immediately.

Molten mozzarella spaghetti

Tuck little cubes of mozzarella into hot tomato-tossed spaghetti and suddenly you've got molten pockets of cheese hiding in every bite. Oregano and parmesan add a familiar, pizza-adjacent vibe. Eat immediately while the mozzarella is still gooey.

Serves 2

200 g (7 oz) dried spaghetti
2 tablespoons extra virgin olive oil
2 garlic cloves, finely chopped
400 g (14 oz) tin Italian roma (plum) tomatoes, whole or crushed
1 teaspoon dried oregano, plus extra to serve
40 g (1/2 cup) freshly grated parmesan, plus extra to serve
100 g (3 1/2 oz) mozzarella, cut into 1.5 cm (1/2 in) cubes, or baby bocconcini

1. Cook the spaghetti in a large saucepan of boiling salted water for about 3 minutes less than specified on the packet, until slightly underdone and less than al dente. Drain.

2. Meanwhile, combine the olive oil and garlic in a deep 28 cm (11 in) unheated frying pan, stirring to coat the garlic with the oil. Cook over medium-low heat for 1–2 minutes, until the garlic is fragrant, swirling the pan regularly.

3. Add the tomatoes and oregano, breaking up the tomatoes with a spoon if they are whole (or with your hands before adding, if you like). Increase the heat to medium-high and simmer for 6–8 minutes, until slightly thickened, stirring occasionally.

4. Add the spaghetti and toss well to completely coat the pasta, shaking the pan and stirring with a wooden spoon for a further 1–2 minutes, to finish cooking the spaghetti and to coat with the sauce.

5. When the pasta is al dente, stir in the parmesan and mozzarella until combined. Taste and season with freshly ground black pepper, and salt if necessary.

6. Divide between warmed serving bowls, ensuring the cheese pieces are tucked inside the spaghetti, to ensure they melt. Sprinkle with extra oregano and parmesan, if you like, and serve immediately.

Cauliflower cheese spaghetti

A comforting twist on a classic combo: cauliflower, cheese and pasta. Here, tender cauliflower is simmered with cream, mustard and cheddar, then simply tossed through slippery spaghetti and crowned with crispy panko breadcrumbs for some satisfying crunch, making this a dish you'll come back to on repeat.

Serves 2

200 g (7 oz) dried spaghetti
3 tablespoons extra virgin olive oil
20 g (1/3 cup) panko breadcrumbs
300 g (10 1/2 oz) cauliflower, cut into small florets
125 ml (1/2 cup) cream (35% fat)
1 1/2 teaspoons dijon mustard
60 g (1/2 cup) grated extra-tasty cheddar, plus extra to serve

1. Cook the spaghetti in a large saucepan of boiling salted water for about 3 minutes less than specified on the packet, until slightly underdone and less than al dente. Scoop out and reserve 250 ml (1 cup) of the pasta water and drain the pasta.

2. Meanwhile, heat 1 tablespoon of the olive oil in a deep 28 cm (11 in) frying pan over medium–high heat. Add the panko breadcrumbs and a good pinch of salt and cook, stirring, for 2–3 minutes, until golden. Transfer to a plate and set aside.

3. Add the remaining oil and the cauliflower to the frying pan. Cover and cook, stirring occasionally, for 5–7 minutes, until the cauliflower is lightly browned and tender–crisp.

4. Add 125 ml (1/2 cup) of the reserved pasta water, along with the cream and mustard. Stir well, bring to the boil, then reduce the heat to a simmer.

5. Add the spaghetti and cheddar to the pan. Stir with a wooden spoon until the cheese melts into the sauce, then cook for 3–5 minutes, stirring and shaking the pan until the pasta is al dente, and the sauce has thickened slightly and coats the pasta. Taste and season with salt and freshly ground black pepper.

6. Divide between warmed serving bowls. Grate some extra cheese over the top, sprinkle with the crispy panko crumbs and serve immediately.

FLORIAN HOME

Spaghetti with chicken katsu golden curry

Crunchy katsu on top, golden Japanese curry sauce underneath – this pasta is comfort food in full colour. Peas add sweetness, sesame seeds a slight nuttiness, and together it's a hug in a bowl.

Serves 2

200 g (7 oz) dried spaghetti
2 tablespoons vegetable oil
2 small crumbed chicken fillets
140 g (1 cup) frozen baby peas
40 g (1½ oz) Japanese curry sauce mix (curry roux blocks), crumbled
1 spring onion (scallion), finely sliced, to serve
toasted black sesame seeds, to serve

1. Cook the spaghetti in a large saucepan of boiling salted water for about 3 minutes less than specified on the packet, until slightly underdone and less than al dente. Scoop out and reserve 375ml (1½ cups) of the pasta water and drain the pasta.

2. Meanwhile, heat the vegetable oil in a deep 28 cm (11 in) frying pan over medium heat. Add the crumbed chicken and cook for 6–8 minutes, until the chicken is golden and cooked through, turning halfway through and adding a little more oil if necessary. Transfer to a warmed plate, cover loosely to keep warm and set aside.

3. Reduce the heat to medium–low and wipe out the pan. Add 250 ml (1 cup) of the reserved pasta water to the pan, along with the peas and curry sauce mix. Stir until the sauce mix dissolves.

4. Add the spaghetti and toss well to combine and coat the pasta, shaking the pan and stirring with a wooden spoon for a further 1–2 minutes, to finish cooking the spaghetti. Add a little more pasta water to thin the sauce if necessary.

5. Divide between warmed serving bowls. Slice the chicken and place on top. Scatter with the spring onion and sesame seeds and serve immediately.

Smoky roasted red pepper spaghetti

Roasted red peppers and paprika create a sweet, smoky sauce that clings to spaghetti with the help of parmesan, creating something that feels both rustic and restaurant-y. Basil on top keeps things fresh, but really, this is comfort food with a sultry streak.

Serves 2

200 g (7 oz) dried spaghetti
2 tablespoons extra virgin olive oil
250 g (9 oz) roasted red bell pepper (capsicum), finely diced
2 garlic cloves, finely chopped
1/2 teaspoon smoked paprika
60 g (3/4 cup) very finely grated parmesan, plus extra to serve
handful fresh basil leaves, to serve

1. Cook the spaghetti in a large saucepan of boiling salted water for about 3 minutes less than specified on the packet, until slightly underdone and less than al dente. Scoop out and reserve 250 ml (1 cup) of the pasta water and drain the pasta.

2. About 6 minutes before the spaghetti is ready, combine the olive oil, roasted pepper, garlic and paprika in a deep 28 cm (11 in) unheated frying pan, stirring to coat the ingredients with the oil. Cook over medium heat for 4–5 minutes, until the garlic is fragrant, stirring often.

3. Add about 125 ml (1/2 cup) of the reserved pasta water and the spaghetti. Toss well to coat the pasta, shaking the pan and stirring with a wooden spoon for a further 1–2 minutes, to finish cooking the spaghetti and to emulsify the pan juices and pasta water. Add a little more pasta water if the mixture seems dry.

4. Remove from the heat, add the parmesan and stir quickly until the cheese melts and the sauce is creamy. Taste and season with freshly ground black pepper, and salt if necessary.

5. Divide between warmed serving bowls, scatter with the basil and serve immediately, with extra parmesan, if you like.

Creamy pumpkin & leek spaghetti

Pumpkin and leek come together here in sweet and savoury harmony. Cooked until tender, they meld with a touch of cream and parmesan into a golden, velvety sauce. Tossed with spaghetti, this is a simple, warming dish that feels light enough for everyday but cosy enough to relish on a chilly night.

Serves 2

200 g (7 oz) dried spaghetti
30 g (1 oz) butter
2 tablespoons extra virgin olive oil
1 leek, white and pale green sections finely sliced
200 g (7 oz) peeled and coarsely grated pumpkin
80 g (1/3 cup) sour cream or cream (35% fat)
25 g (1/3 cup) very finely grated parmesan, plus extra to serve

1. Cook the spaghetti in a large saucepan of boiling salted water for about 3 minutes less than specified on the packet, until slightly underdone and less than al dente. Scoop out and reserve 250 ml (1 cup) of the pasta water and drain the pasta.

2. Meanwhile, heat the butter and oil in a deep 28 cm (11 in) frying pan over medium heat. Add the leek, pumpkin and a good pinch of salt. Cover and cook, stirring occasionally, for 6–8 minutes, until the vegetables are tender.

3. Add the sour cream and about 125 ml (1/2 cup) of the reserved pasta water. Bring to the boil, then reduce the heat to a simmer.

4. Add the spaghetti and parmesan to the pan. Stir with a wooden spoon until the cheese melts into the sauce, then cook for 1–2 minutes, stirring and shaking the pan until the pasta is al dente, and the sauce has thickened slightly and coats the pasta. Taste and season with salt and freshly ground black pepper.

5. Divide between warmed serving bowls, grate some more parmesan over the top and serve immediately.

Deli spaghetti

Everything you love from the deli counter, tossed with spaghetti and called dinner. Salami sizzles in olive oil, roasted peppers bring sweetness, semi-dried tomatoes add tang, artichokes keep it classy and parmesan pulls it all together into a salty, glossy sauce. It's basically an antipasto platter that figured out carbs were the missing link.

Serves 2

200 g (7 oz) dried spaghetti
2 tablespoons extra virgin olive oil
100 g (3½ oz) sliced salami, cut into strips
100 g (3½ oz) roasted red bell pepper (capsicum), cut into strips
100 g (3½ oz) drained semi-dried or sun-dried tomatoes in oil, roughly chopped
2 artichoke hearts about 60 g (2 oz), finely sliced
40 g (½ cup) very finely grated parmesan, plus extra to serve

1. Cook the spaghetti in a large saucepan of boiling salted water for about 3 minutes less than specified on the packet, until slightly underdone and less than al dente. Scoop out and reserve 250 ml (1 cup) of the pasta water and drain the pasta.

2. Meanwhile, heat the olive oil and salami in a deep 28 cm (11 in) unheated frying pan, stirring to coat the salami with the oil. Cook over medium heat for 3–5 minutes, swirling the pan and stirring regularly, until the salami starts to lightly brown. Add the roasted pepper strips, tomato and artichoke and cook, stirring, for 2 minutes, or until heated through.

3. Add 125 ml (½ cup) of the reserved pasta water and the spaghetti. Toss well to coat the pasta, shaking the pan and stirring with a wooden spoon for a further 1–2 minutes, to finish cooking the spaghetti and to emulsify the pan juices and pasta water. Add a little more pasta water if the mixture seems dry.

4. Remove the pan from the heat and add the parmesan. Stir, shaking the pan, until melted and combined to make a creamy sauce. Taste and season generously with freshly ground black pepper, and salt if necessary.

5. Divide between warmed serving bowls and serve immediately, with extra parmesan.

PET NAT

Spaghetti naporitan

A retro post-war classic from Japan that tastes like childhood in pasta form. Tumbled with undeniably tasty frankfurts and tangy peppers, spaghetti is doused in a deliciously glossy ketchup sauce with a cheeky sprinkling of parmesan – perfect for a merry late-night dinner dash down memory lane.

Serves 2

200 g (7 oz) dried spaghetti
1 tablespoon vegetable oil
250 g (9 oz) skinless frankfurts, sliced diagonally
1 small green bell pepper (capsicum), cut to a similar size as the frankfurts
80 ml (1/3 cup) tomato ketchup (a Japanese one, if available)
1 teaspoon worcestershire sauce or Japanese soy sauce
40 g (1/2 cup) very finely grated parmesan, plus extra to serve

1. Cook the spaghetti in a large saucepan of boiling salted water for about 3 minutes less than specified on the packet, until slightly underdone and less than al dente. Scoop out and reserve 250 ml (1 cup) of the pasta water and drain the pasta.

2. Meanwhile, heat the vegetable oil in a deep 28 cm (11 in) frying pan over medium–high heat. Add the frankfurt and green pepper slices and cook for 3–5 minutes, stirring regularly, until the sausage starts to brown and the green pepper softens slightly.

3. Reduce the heat to medium and stir in the ketchup and worcestershire or soy sauce. Add 125 ml (1/2 cup) of the reserved pasta water and the spaghetti. Toss well to coat the pasta, shaking the pan and stirring with a wooden spoon for a further 1–2 minutes, to finish cooking the spaghetti and form the sauce. Add a little more pasta water if the mixture seems dry.

4. Remove the pan from the heat and add the parmesan. Stir, shaking the pan, until melted and combined. Taste and season generously with freshly ground black pepper, and salt if necessary.

5. Divide between warmed serving bowls, top with extra parmesan and serve immediately.

'Marry me' chicken spaghetti

They say this pasta is so good it could seal the deal – tender chicken, tangy sour cream, loads of sun-dried tomatoes and parmesan all tangled up in a slippery sauce. Rich, ravishing and a little dramatic, it's definitely date-night material.

Serves 2

200 g (7 oz) dried spaghetti
1 tablespoon oil (from the sun-dried tomatoes below)
250 g (9 oz) chicken tenderloins
150 g (5½ oz) drained plump sun-dried tomatoes in oil, roughly chopped
125 g (½ cup) sour cream
2 teaspoons dijon mustard
40 g (½ cup) finely grated parmesan, plus extra to serve

1. Cook the spaghetti in a large saucepan of boiling salted water for about 3 minutes less than specified on the packet, until slightly underdone and less than al dente. Scoop out and reserve 250 ml (1 cup) of the pasta water and drain the pasta.

2. Heat the oil in a deep 28 cm (11 in) frying pan over medium heat. Season the chicken with a good pinch of salt, then cook for 5–6 minutes, turning occasionally, until the chicken is golden and just cooked through. Transfer to a warmed plate and cover to keep warm.

3. Add the tomatoes to the pan, along with the sour cream, mustard and 125 ml (½ cup) of the reserved pasta water. Stir well and bring to the boil, then reduce the heat to a simmer.

4. Add the spaghetti and parmesan to the pan. Stir with a wooden spoon until the cheese melts into the sauce, then cook for 1–2 minutes, stirring and shaking the pan until the sauce is slightly thickened and coats the pasta.

5. Slice the chicken and stir it all in, adding a little more pasta water to thin the sauce if necessary. Taste and season with salt and freshly ground black pepper.

6. Divide between warmed serving bowls or plates, grate some more parmesan over the top and serve immediately.

& DICE
Issue No. 23
Cooks
Cooks
A Catalan classic revised, iconic Detroit snacks, a sweet surprise from Russia—recipes from legendary restaurants worldwide.
Get lost in flavour

Salmon with miso butter spaghetti

Silky miso butter and parmesan meet tender salmon and bok choy for a dish that feels like comfort food with a Japanese accent. Creamy, savoury and just a little luxurious.

Serves 2

200 g (7 oz) dried spaghetti
1 teaspoon extra virgin olive oil
200 g (7 oz) skinless salmon fillet, pin bones removed, flesh cut into 2.5 cm (1 in) chunks
30 g (1 oz) butter
1 tablespoon miso paste (see Tip)
2 heads of baby bok choy (pak choy), finely sliced
40 g (1/2 cup) finely grated parmesan, plus extra to serve

1. Cook the spaghetti in a large saucepan of boiling salted water for about 3 minutes less than specified on the packet, until slightly underdone and less than al dente. Scoop out and reserve 375 ml (1 1/2 cups) water and drain the pasta.

2. About 6 minutes before the spaghetti is ready, heat the olive oil in a deep 28 cm (11 in) frying pan over medium–high heat. Add the salmon and cook, turning regularly for 3–5 minutes, until golden all over, but not cooked through. Transfer to a plate, cover to keep warm and set aside.

3. Add 185 ml (3/4 cup) of the reserved pasta water to the pan, along with the butter and miso paste. Stir well until combined, bring to the boil, then reduce the heat to a simmer.

4. Add the spaghetti and bok choy. Toss well to coat the pasta, shaking the pan and stirring with a wooden spoon for a further 1–2 minutes, to finish cooking the spaghetti, wilt the bok choy and emulsify the sauce. Add a little more pasta water if the mixture seems dry.

5. Remove the pan from the heat and add the parmesan. Stir, shaking the pan, until melted and combined. Flake the salmon and gently stir it into the spaghetti mixture to coat with the sauce.

6. Divide between warmed serving bowls, grate some extra parmesan over the top and serve immediately.

Tip

Miso is a fermented soy bean paste. Shiro (white) miso is milder than aka (red) miso, which is deeper in flavour as it has been fermented for longer. You can use either in this recipe.

VICTORIA

Spaghetti with Italian sausage meatballs

Shortcut meatballs! Just squeeze sausage meat from its casing, roll into bite-sized chunks, then sizzle until browned. Kale and tomato pasta sauce join the party, silky spaghetti gets tossed right in, and suddenly you've got a pasta dish that feels like you've put in the effort, without actually requiring any. Parmesan on top, always. This is weeknight comfort disguised as late-night indulgence.

Serves 2

200 g (7 oz) dried spaghetti
1 tablespoon extra virgin olive oil
250 g (9 oz) Italian-style pork and fennel sausages
4 large cavolo nero or curly kale leaves, stalks stripped, leaves roughly torn
400 g (14 oz) jar good-quality tomato pasta sauce
freshly grated parmesan, to serve

1. Cook the spaghetti in a large saucepan of boiling salted water for about 3 minutes less than specified on the packet, until slightly underdone and less than al dente. Drain.

2. Meanwhile, heat the olive oil in a deep 28 cm (11 in) frying pan over medium–high heat. Squeeze the sausage meat out of the skins in small ball shapes and add to the pan. Shake the pan to coat the meatballs with the oil. Cook for 3–5 minutes, shaking the pan regularly, until the meatballs are well browned, but not cooked through.

3. Add the kale and stir for a minute or two until the kale starts to wilt. Pour in the tomato sauce, bring to a simmer and cook, stirring occasionally, for about 3 minutes, until the kale is tender. Taste and season with salt and freshly ground black pepper.

4. Add the spaghetti and toss well to coat the pasta, shaking the pan and stirring with a wooden spoon for a further 1–2 minutes, to finish cooking the spaghetti.

5. Divide between warmed serving bowls, top with a generous sprinkling of parmesan and serve.

Vegemite & cheese spaghetti

When the pantry shelves are almost bare, this is comfort food with a distinctively Aussie twist – just spaghetti, butter, garlic, tomato paste, a cheeky spoonful of Vegemite and plenty of cheese to finish. Salty, savoury and oddly addictive, this warm and satisfying no-fuss dish will save the day when those late-night hunger pangs hit.

Serves 2

200 g (7 oz) dried spaghetti
2 tablespoons extra virgin olive oil
30 g (1 oz) butter
2 garlic cloves, finely chopped
2 teaspoons Vegemite
2 teaspoons tomato paste (concentrated puree)
grated cheddar, to serve

1. Cook the spaghetti in a large saucepan of boiling salted water for about 3 minutes less than specified on the packet, until slightly underdone and less than al dente. Scoop out and reserve 250 ml (1 cup) of the pasta water and drain the pasta.

2. Combine the olive oil, butter and garlic in a deep 28 cm (11 in) unheated frying pan. Cook over low heat for 1–2 minutes, swirling the pan regularly, until the garlic is fragrant. Stir in the Vegemite and tomato paste and cook, stirring, for a further minute, until the Vegemite dissolves into the sauce.

3. Add about 125 ml (1/2 cup) of the reserved pasta water and the spaghetti. Toss well to coat the pasta, shaking the pan and stirring with a wooden spoon for a further 1–2 minutes, to finish cooking the spaghetti and to emulsify the pan juices and pasta water. Add a little more pasta water if the mixture seems dry.

4. Divide between warmed serving bowls or plates. Scatter with grated cheddar and serve immediately.

Tanqueray
LONDON DRY GIN
CAMPARI
MILANO
MONKEY 47
Amaro
MONTENEGRO
1885
BARDINET
CRÈME DE CASSIS DE DIJON
D.O.M
BENEDICTINE

Index

SHADY